What a Difference a Day Makes!

JANET HANNA

ISBN 978-1-63575-031-7 (Paperback)
ISBN 978-1-63575-032-4 (Digital)

Christian Faith Publishing, Inc.
296 Chestnut Street
Meadville, PA 16335
www.christianfaithpublishing.com

Printed in the United States of America

"*You have turned my mourning into joyful dancing, You have taken away my clothes of mourning and clothed me with joy, that I might sing praises to you and not be silent. O LORD my God, I will give you thanks forever*" (Psalm 30:11–12, NLT).

Dedication

I dedicate this book to my Lord and Savior Jesus Christ, because apart from Him, this would not have been possible!

Introduction

Everyone has a desire to be wanted and loved. However, in the pursuit of love and happiness, we make decisions that change our lives forever.

God placed a void on the inside of every human being. He reaches out to mankind in countless ways, longing to fill the hungry soul. It is God's desire to complete us—spirit, soul, and body. However, that completion can only come through a personal relationship with His Son, Jesus Christ.

One day, I discovered that it was possible to be happy in spite of circumstances. That realization came on April 6, 1996, when I accepted Jesus Christ as my personal Lord and Savior. The warmth of His love filled my soul. A heart that was once sorrowful had become joyful because of my newfound freedom in Christ.

This book is an attempt to describe my continuing journey with God. It is my hope that others will see that God can cause them to smile from the inside out—in spite of circumstances!

My prayer is that all who read this book will be encouraged, knowing that it is not how we start that determines how we will finish. But true success is found as we yield our will to Jesus Christ. At that place, He will finish all that He began in our lives and we will say with certainty, "What a difference a day makes!"

Contents

My Father's Love

In my weakness, God reached down to me with love
Believing that from my pitiful state, I could rise above
God's love for me was proven before I would exist
Saturating me with tenderness, although I would resist

Disguising my pain and longing to feel whole
As my life fell apart and spun out of control
Watching in horror as my life would unfold
In the clutches of darkness, caught in its hold

Pretending to be happy, but feeling out of place
Trying to fit in, wearing a mask over my face
Behind closed doors, my heart would break
With emptiness inside, it continued to ache

God refused to let go, but tenderly embraced me
Wiping my tears, so determined to set me free
He saw life's disappointments that were deep inside
Sadness overshadowed me, I could no longer hide

In the midst of living, the emptiness did not leave
Though bitter and broken, to sin I would cleave
In my defiance, mercy fought and chased after me
Rebuking the blindness, convinced I would see

At the appointed time, God's soldiers were in place
Praying for me, believing I too would join the race
With fervent love, God pursued me, refusing to quit
Knowing that one day, to Him I would submit

The years have passed and I look back in awe
That hanging on the cross, I know who Jesus saw
Now with all my heart, I thank heaven above
That my most precious gift is My Father's love

I Believe

Society continues to deny Almighty God
Yet life without Him leaves an eternal void
The world is filled with so much despair
Burdens are heavy and happiness is rare

America has forgotten her Christian roots
To every shameful act, she stands and salutes
Morals are foreign to our native land
To simply exist was never God's plan

Peace and tranquility, no one can conceive
Yet in one Lord, one Savior, I believe
Consider His works, ponder His grace
Sins washed away without one trace

Jesus freely died that we might live
He is quick to love and eager to forgive
Apart from Christ, we are never complete
But miserable, confused, and full of defeat

Lost and without hope until Love awakens us
Set free from bondage when in God we trust
Jesus gave us new life, He gave us His peace
His blood won our liberty, He paid for our release

Each day, God unveils heavenly success
As we hold on to the hope that we profess
Changed on the inside, born from above
Lifted out of darkness, hidden in God's love

Hope will be found by those with a hungry heart
Standing on the promise of a brand-new start
Wisdom is laid up for those who will seek it out
Trusting in God's Word, staying far from doubt

God opens His heart and allows us to look inside
In Him we find safety, a place that we can hide
Calling us to His side—our reason for living
The message of hope, God keeps on giving

Jesus will return in the clouds on high
Piercing the darkness, lighting the sky
Bidding us to come to the Wedding Feast
The first shall be last and the greatest the least

I knew only darkness until Christ came
Life since then has never been the same
The splendors of heaven, I will someday receive
Unashamedly proclaiming, in Jesus I believe

Dancing with Jesus

Lord, teach me to trust Your unfailing love
My candle in the dark, my beam from above

Keep me close, hidden under Your wings
Help me surrender all earthly things

Made complete as I look upon Your face
Hidden in Your heart, within that secret place

Nothing else matters when I am at Your side
In the center of Your heart, I long to abide

Dancing by the moonlit sky, nothing is dearer
Never wanting to leave, only drawing nearer

The rhythm of our hearts fills the night air
Lost in Your love, there's none to compare

Gliding under the stars, forgetting earth's pain
Basking in Your presence, caught in heaven's rain

The sunrise announces a brand-new day
Cooing away the night, extending my stay

In You, I am drenched, how refreshing it is
Delighting in You, sealed in heaven's bliss

Amazing me with wonders yet untold
Hushing my fears and calming my soul

Running in the night, chasing the essence of You
Enjoying this moment, my dream has come true

Lingering for a while, not wanting to leave
Elated in You, so grateful that I believe

Capturing each second and holding it tightly
Ascending to the heavens, rising ever so slightly

Reaching for the stars, seeing them in view
Listening to the breeze, enjoying it anew

Treasuring my Love, simply enjoying Him
The cares of the world have become quite dim

Capturing the moment, enjoying heaven's tune
Dancing under the stars by the light of the moon

The sky and stars are a beautiful sight to behold
Daybreak tells a lovely story, and I watch it unfold

You hold my hand and cause the darkness to disappear
Sweetly reminding me that Your return is drawing near

Dancing across the floors of heaven, not missing a beat
Your heavenly countenance is so fair and so sweet

You saturate my soul and leave me complete
I have longed for this day that we would meet

With wonder and amazement, I am enraptured
My heart and my soul, You have captured

With great joy and delight, my heart begins to sing
Bowing before my Lord, my Master, and my King

Tears stream down as I comprehend it all
A moment like this, I have no other to recall

In the secret place, You watch over me
Your mercy and grace that I might see

For You are my beloved and my Light
So far beyond the grasp of earthly sight

Lord, give me a new song to sing to You
Filled with praise and worship, this renew

Purposing to know and esteem Your ways
Vowing to honor You all of my days

I collapse in Your arms, never wanting to leave
Under the shadow of the Almighty, I desire to cleave

Praying for others and yearning for them to see
The freedom that I found when You saved me

Saturated by You as I thirst for more
My Savior, my Lord, it is You that I adore

The sweetness of Your presence bids me come
In Your dwelling place is where I find my home

Writing the pages of time here on earth
Revealing Your love, giving us new birth

Satisfied in Your presence and soaring far above
Quieted in Your sanctuary, in awe of Your love

Hidden in Your heart, kept safe in Your embrace
Dancing with You, Jesus, beholding Your face

Finding Hope in Brokenness

Things of this life are not meant for us to hold
We must surrender everything to God's control

Let go of the reins and freely release it all
Open your ears, for the Spirit does call

The cares of this world can sadden a face
Yet in our weakness we receive God's grace

Instead of condemnation, we receive love
Forgiveness and mercy from heaven above

God gives us road maps along the way
Safe from harm, He longs for us to stay

Dependence on God is not half-hearted
It's full speed ahead once we've started

Like sheep, we are clueless on our own
Needing the Shepherd to set the tone

Tossed to and fro by the demands of life
Surrounded by bitterness and unending strife

Facing each day as if it were our own
Yet for many joy and peace is still unknown

Learning life's lessons can ease the pain
When wisdom and truth we purpose to gain

It's when we are broken that we become whole
Watching the Master's plan so sweetly unfold

Finding hope in brokenness is within sight
When we seek God's heart with all of our might

The Gift of Motherhood

Whether playing with trains or caring for colds
The gift of motherhood abundantly unfolds

Watching children grow before our eyes
Cherishing today, for how quickly time flies

Brushing his teeth or combing her hair
Enjoying simple things, not having a care

Learning the alphabet and counting to ten
With shouts of "I did it!" with a clap and a grin

The love of a child produces its own rewards
Like pet bugs and rocks and Mother's Day cards

Valuing that which is lost in everyday living
Like laughter, big dreams, and freely giving

Yes, God has blessed mothers in a special way
Reminding us of His love each and every day

Through the love of a child, joy is truly understood
It is nurtured and cherished throughout motherhood

The Rainbow Is a Circle

Life has so many twists and turns
With things coming at us from all directions
At the end of one adventure, another unfolds
We fail to see God's beauty in our everyday lives
Like the brilliant array of colors found in a rainbow
It is a portrait painted by God, etched across the sky
Symbolizing something beautiful and everlasting
The rainbow is a sign of God's covenant love
Such love has no beginning and it has no end
We try to find fulfillment in the things of the world
In search of that pot of gold, we find ourselves disillusioned
When we come to the end of ourselves, God wraps us in Himself
At that place, the rainbow never ends, for it is a circle

Teach Me to Number My Days

Lord, teach me to number my days as I should
Learning from the bad times, cherishing the good
Appreciating every day that I am blessed to know
Doing Your will, expressing gratitude as I go

Use my life to show others that You are real
As I serve You with joy and fulfill Your will
May I treasure every moment that this life brings
Seeing the hand of God and accepting all things

God knows and He cares, His Son bears the scars
He is not blind to our struggles and internal wars

There is much to be thankful for in this walk of life
Kept free from the bondage of misery and strife

Called to proclaim truth as we patiently wait
For our real reward just beyond heaven's gate
My heart's cry is to be faithful with every day
Purposing to love God, to watch, and to pray

My life is in God's hands, my future is bright
Looking through the eyes of faith, not by sight
Knowing that I am His gives me great peace
Safe in His arms, to Jesus my cares I release

This world has no hope if we refuse to share
That Jesus loves people, He carries every care
Lord, enlarge my vision that I will clearly see
This world is hurting, lift my eyes beyond me

Give me a strong desire to see others succeed
Bring peace to others, as You meet every need
Letting go of the past, that the future I might gain
Always aware of my days, not running in vain

Remembering God's Goodness

Lord, thank You for the gift of each new day
I am blessed beyond measure along the way
Trusting in Your goodness, mercy, and grace
Guided by Your hand, as I run this race

So many times, there seemed no way through
Yet without fail, You spoke what I should do
Not depend on my own strength, but trust in You
To make each day fresh and start it anew

I sometimes wander and take the wrong road
Carrying my burdens, overcome by the load
Like a Father who loves and only wants His best
Your heart longs to see me in the place of rest

Allowing me to make mistakes, doing as I will
Knowing that which I seek, only You can fulfill
Sheltering me with love, applying healing balm
That which was stormy, in Your presence is calm

There is none to compare, no other is dearer
To your blood-stained cross, Lord, draw me nearer
My desire is to love You with all of my heart
Staying faithful to You, never wanting to depart

The debt for sin was more than I could pay
But through the blood of Jesus, God made a way
Because I am blessed by Your merciful ways
I will remember Your goodness all of my days

Laying It All Down

Christ makes it possible to smile, in the midst of pain
The world doesn't understand; to them, this is insane

He enables us to comfort others in our distress
For in reaching out to others, our burdens become less

Finding peace beyond life's valleys and hills
With strength and hope, weary souls God fills

Encouraging others, as we are strengthened in the Lord
Overjoyed, as the love of God to others we freely afford

Getting beyond ourselves is a never-ending story
Ever learning that it is Christ in us, the hope of glory

By God's grace, we make progress along the way
As His amazing love overcomes fear and dismay

When we lose ourselves, in Christ, we are found
Bearing other's burdens, as we lay ours down

Bowing before our Master, on our knees we rise
In this place of surrender is where our purpose lies

Reassured of the Father's love for all mankind
He gives strength to the weak and sight to the blind

In a world of uncertainty, our hope remains strong
With a sweet song from heaven to carry us along

That place of rest in Jesus, others too will find
As we lay it all down and allow Christ to shine

The Way Up Is Down

Worries are few when standing on top of the mountain
As blessings flow freely from heaven's open fountain

That we are blessed to be a blessing is seldom heard
We have taken it lightly; we have ignored God's Word

Preoccupied with bigger barns, we are on the verge of a fall
Consumed with ourselves, while on God we refuse to call

Like flowers in a field, worldly riches will fade away
And that which is real will stand on Judgment Day

In our quest for more, we ignore God, Who gives to all
Proclaiming our self-worth, determined to stand tall

In our self-exalted state, we have reached the lowest place
Still, mercy fights to save us from the sorrow we will face

With a heart full of compassion, God patiently waits
Bidding us to come, swinging open heaven's gates

Many times, we are brought low that we might rise
Needing to lose ourselves and see through God's eyes

In hard times, we struggle to see through the storm
Forgetting that we are in Christ, kept safe from harm

Grace and mercy awaits, if on our knees we will fall
Knowing that God is with us, attentive to every call

When we bow our hearts to God, we are no longer bound
But find freedom in knowing that the way up is down

The Grace to See the Best in Others

God grants us grace to see the best in others
Seeing beyond attitudes, whimpering, and whining
Taking the time to love and care for children
Standing in the gap for many fathers and mothers

In order to grant the wish of one small child,
We must let go of our agendas and make time for others
By reading a book to a child or helping with a toy
Taking the extra time to get one more smile

The seeds that we sow yield children's genuine love
The ability to see the best in others takes time and patience
Not focusing on the negative, but embracing the positive
This is a noteworthy trait, a gift from God above

We must look at a child and see a bright, shining star
Not fixed on the present, but seeing where they can be
That's how God sees us, polished and brand-new
As new creations in Christ, for that's what we are

The time that we spend to teach others in time will tell
God always rewards our faithfulness to fulfill His purposes
He granted us an awesome responsibility in caring for children
And with His help, we will stay the course and finish well

Surrender My Plans

Another year has come and gone
And I ponder seeds that I have sown

Moving forward with a grateful heart
Knowing that each Red Sea, God will part

Like a flower that blooms, then fades away
So does tomorrow as it becomes yesterday

Learning to walk by patience's voice
Carefully weighing each earthly choice

Leaning on God, not standing on my own
That at the end of each test, I will have grown

As God is eternal and does not change
My life I must adjust, my plans rearrange

I must surrender my plans and let God be
Embracing His will, as He consumes me

The Love of God

The love of God endures forever, it will not end
Marred and broken lives, God continues to mend
With a mighty hand, He delivers us from despair
The hearts of hurting people, God longs to repair

Take time to consider all that God has done
Remember countless battles that He has won
Leading us by the hand, and showing us the way
Speaking words to encourage throughout each day

God supplies our needs, as we seek Him first
He waters the dry places and quenches our thirst
God's power goes beyond our man-made walls
With unconditional love, to every sinner He calls

At the throne of grace, in Christ made new
Looking to Jesus, for He is faithful and true
We experience our Father's love like never before
As we surrender to Jesus, God's only open door

Jesus is the greatest Gift, God's precious Gem
Our sins are erased, as we put our trust in Him
We are blessed with a Lord, a Savior, and a Friend
As mercy cries out, the love of God will never end

Gratitude

Looking toward heaven, we raise our hands
Gazing upward, forgetting life's demands

Believing God's plan and trusting His ways
Yielding our will, releasing our praise

Blessed without measure by the Master's touch
That which seems small, God always makes much

We look to the cross and leave burdens there
As we walk by faith, giving God every care

Hidden in God, with mindful purpose we stay
As He orders our steps throughout each day

We share heaven's treasure with others in need
Assured that by God's Word, others He will feed

Every life is precious and should not be wasted
As the blessings of God, we've all richly tasted

Strengthened by faith, through the Lord becoming bold
Mindful of God's unwavering hand, as His plans unfold

Anticipating tomorrow, toward heaven we face
With joy from above, that no earthly care can erase

With heartfelt thanks for the gift called today
We express our gratitude, as we kneel and pray

My Hiding Place

Though the storms rage, I have a hiding place
Safe and secure, wrapped in God's embrace
This is the place that I can finally be free
Where God brings peace and gently quiets me

He silences my mind and helps me forget today
Giving me sweet serenity, as I kneel and pray
Removing distractions that I may hear clearly
Reminding me again how He loves me dearly

Though I encounter battles along the way
I am shielded by God, equipped each day
Running ahead because I am destined to win
With power from above, no longer held by sin

Finding a life with ease when I stay in the nest
Yet God encourages me to fly, for He knows best
Within the safe zone, there is not much to lose
But walking by faith is what I must choose

Reminded that the lighthouse is still in view
Guiding my steps, showing me what to do
God's will becomes mine, as I look into His face
Surrendered to Him, safe in my hiding place

Completely His

It's easy to make promises deep inside the fire
Running to God when circumstances are dire

Depending on ourselves when resources are at hand
Quickly retreating when we've done all that we can

Halfheartedly coming to the One Who redeems
Vowing to submit to God, or so it seems

Casually committing that which we fail to yield
For what God wants most is our surrendered will

Never finding that place of peace on our own
Because God never meant for us to go it alone

Only God can complete us, as we yield to Him
Molded by the Potter, shaped into a precious gem

Determined that God's plans, we won't miss
No longer adrift, but finally completely His

This Final Hour

Hanging from a rope, thinking it is secure
Holding on to things which are so unsure

Clueless about the hour that we call today
Following after Balaam, forever going astray

As love chases us, we wait for yet another day
Heading in the opposite direction, farther away

With blinders over our eyes, we refuse to see
Bowing to Satan, a puppet for his every plea

Down on our knees, we purpose not to fall
Looking to others, yet on God refusing to call

The hour is late and the sun will soon set
As many side with Satan, held in his debt

The hand of God is patient, but will soon lift
As Jesus has been sent, God's most precious Gift

We fail to see tomorrow and all that is ahead
As we succumb to the flesh, and by it are led

Mercy cries out for us to live holy and just
Saying run after God and flee worldly lust

Much work remains and there is not much time
As the sound of heaven's clock prepares to chime

Fall on your face and repent with a sincere heart
For God promises forgiveness, a brand-new start

God sends His messengers again and again
Bidding all to accept Jesus, to heed His plan

Turn from sin and be washed in Jesus's blood
Safe from harm, set free from hell's flood

Jesus loves us so much more than we know
Kindness and compassion, He longs to show

God longs to free mankind from Satan's power
If we will cry out to Him in this final hour

He Hears My Heart

When the world comes crashing down on me
And I look to God to hear my desperate plea

When the pressure seems too much to bear
And hope that thrived has turned to despair

When my faith is small and I doubt my way
And dreams are shattered, leaving only dismay

When I search God's Word, but fail to see
And struggle with the person He's called me to be

When peace is present, but fear longs to abide
And there is no place to escape, nowhere to hide

When there are no words to describe feelings inside
And the faith of my heart and knowledge collide

When I lift my eyes, believing for God's best
And seek to find that place of unending rest

It is at that place that I trust God to do His part
For He knows my every need—He hears my heart

Time to Be a Child

When I cannot hear beyond the noise of this troubled world
God speaks deep inside of me, and His voice comforts me
As I stare at the ceiling, wondering what tomorrow will bring
He's held me many times, even as I've struggled to run away

In times of anger, my flesh and spirit fight against each other
When patience seems out of reach, God reminds me He is here
When I cannot be strong, God lets me know it's okay to be weak
For that is the place that His strength is brightest for all to see

God knows every detail of my life, He's always known me
My flaws don't cause Him to walk away, only to draw nearer
He holds me tightly and encourages me to give my tears to Him
Showing me over and over that He can be trusted with my heart

God does not search for words to say, as He is the sum of all words
When nothing makes sense, God's faithfulness is always certain
When I need rest from this busy world, I lay my head on God's heart
Because the answers that I seek are waiting for me in that place

Before time existed, God knew me, loved me, and ordained me
When I fall, He reminds me that it's not how I started that counts
He cheers me on, thoroughly convinced that I can and will rise again
Freely forgetting the mistakes of my past and covering them with love

When my head forgets, my heart reminds me that Jesus is here
Giving me the desire to go on, to be that person that others see
A lover of God, steadfast, devoted, a faithful warrior for Him
Ever living to please Him, running in the strength of the Lord

Many see me standing and don't know the One Who holds me up
They don't know the times that I've questioned God's next step
Hanging on to hope, wondering what the future has in store
Still others see maturity in the midst of my struggle with growth

Sometimes I long for sight, as I trust the Lord to order my steps
To be seen for who I am—a lover of God, yet quite human
As God continues to mold and mature the person that others see
I am grateful that in His presence, there is still time to be a child

My Faithful Friend

Through the ups and downs, He's been there
A way in the wilderness, He would prepare

As I've journeyed down life's winding road
Each time He's been there to carry the load

So often, I've faced yet another Red Sea
Yet Jesus was there, patiently guiding me

Wiping my tears, holding me close to His heart
Each time willing to give me a brand-new start

In difficult times, my Faithful Friend has been there
Loving me, reassuring me that He will always care

During times of celebration, He rejoices with me
Reminding me of the good things I am yet to see

I can always count on the One Who promised to stay
As He faithfully journeys with me each and every day

The Courage to Go On

God grants me grace to face each day
Washing away pain, hurt, and dismay

Allowing me to see life through His eyes
Without pretense, letting go of my disguise

In His presence, I receive wholeness
Faith for today and unhindered boldness

God encourages me to soar high above the earth
Revealing His love, His kindness, and His worth

Holding my hand and steadying my step
Reassuring me that in Him I am kept

Safe in God's care, I am never alone
Because He gives me courage to go on

Help Is on the Way

We often look for others to complete us
Pledging our hearts, to love and to trust

But it is God alone who makes us whole
Filling the emptiness in our thirsty soul

When troubles are high and spirits are low
The throne of grace is where we must go

When a major task is just facing another day
Be encouraged because help is on the way

Reminisce

There is a beautiful place not far from here
Filled with memories that we hold dear

Close your eyes and look with your heart
Find that place where new dreams start

Run through the grass and shuffle your feet
Breathe in the air, smell the flowers so sweet

Go back to that place of simplicity and peace
Where precious moments in time will never cease

The Blessings of Today

The blessings of today are ever before us
Reminding us that in God we must trust

Given new life and placed in God's hands
Getting things in order for His eternal plans

The burdens of life will not weigh our hearts down
If under the shadow of the Almighty, we are found

We must lift our thoughts beyond what we can do
And cast our gaze on Jesus, for He is always in view

Call on His name, For He is never far away
He strengthens our spirits as we kneel and pray

The blessings of today will be plainly seen
If on our Lord, we will continually lean

Racing against Time

The day is gone and the night is far spent
The call has gone out; the message has been sent

Time is of the essence, but people have no clue
Caught up in busyness, not knowing what to do

Disaster is all around and people long to hide
Chaos fills our streets, and fear is on every side

Life's disappointments are written on each face
Yet without hope, people run from place to place

No need for concern is what we continue to say
As time races by and we lose yet another day

A confused world wonders what we are all about
As we quote God's Word, but still live in doubt

As the baton passes by, many turn away
Caught in sin's clutches, choosing to stay

Not counting blessings, but only wanting more
Commanded to be thankful, yet this we ignore

The flame of the Holy Spirit continues to go
Yet we seem oblivious, as if we don't know

The blazing fire of yesterday is now a faint spark
For that which burned brightly has now become dark

The church slumbers and sleeps, as hell enlarges itself
Yet the Word of God is unopened and placed on a shelf

Danger awaits, but who will sound the alarm
Snatching lost souls from impending harm

The Bible fulfills itself, living every word
God's proclamation, by all has been heard

Arise, sleeping giant, hear the Spirit call
Rend your hearts, and on your faces fall

Shake off the dust and ready yourself
Open your ears, refuse to be deaf

Keep God in the center, put Him first
For Him alone, we must hunger and thirst

The day is gone, and the night is far spent
Time races by and there is little time to repent

Joy Comes

Indescribable joy comes as I set at His feet
I am forever changed, in Christ made complete

No earthly treasures I bring to the Mercy Seat
Yet that which I offer is lovely and sweet

That which God desires, I do not fail to see
For it is my life, my love, it is all of me

In this place of worship, I am gloriously filled
Set free, empowered, and spiritually healed

The warmth of God's presence is what I desire
A passion burns inside like an unquenchable fire

Joy comes as I throw off the weight of the world
Basking in the glow of Jesus, my precious Pearl

I am God's songbird, for Him I will always sing
My praise, my life, my everything, I vow to bring

Early in the morning, my heart cries out to Him
My reason for living, my most precious Gem

Joy comes as I refuse to be silent before My King
Enthroning Him on my heart, giving Him everything

For God's Glory and Your Good

Don't be surprised by the tests that come your way
For every bit of pain, God's glory will far outweigh

Keep your heads up, even when you don't understand
In the hard places, God will strengthen your inner man

Being fully persuaded, you will finish the race
With a song in your heart, and a smile on your face

For God has called you for such a time as this
His blessings, His favor, you will not miss

Behind the scenes, you pour out your heart
And the cares of the sheep, from you, never part

Lift up your eyes for many have come to hear
Tell the story of Jesus and how He drew you near

The sheep are listening, they hear the Shepherd's voice
Give them God's Word, for it will seal their eternal choice

The secret place of God is where you've chosen to abide
God honors that, and many things in you, He will confide

Yes, God is working it all out, purposed for your good
With a goal in mind, He performs the process as He should

Many times you've asked if there are ears that hear
Desiring the hearts of others to hold your Savior dear

But be encouraged, servants of God, for He does see
And as you cry out to Him, many are being set free

Though the battles have been fierce, there is a reason
God has readied you, prepared you for this new season

Many will come to know the Christ that you dearly love
For much prayer has been sowed, it's been echoed above

As God makes adjustments, you choose to remain
Staying faithful to Him, for nothing is done in vain

Continue on the narrow path, looking to God as you should
And God's plan will be worked, for His glory and your good

Praise with a Price

There is praise that comes from a deeper place
Where the cares of this world will never erase

Like unopened perfume that is placed on a shelf
The fragrance is there, yet alone, left to itself

The bottle is opened, and the aroma is revealed
Releasing the sweetness of what was concealed

This praise is not defined, and it's never on queue
It is never rehearsed but alive, festive, and new

Praise with a price is most precious and quite rare
Coming from within, where the soul is laid bare

This praise reverberates long after others are gone
In the quiet times with Jesus, set apart and alone

As we rend our hearts, God's will is made clear
And we listen to God's Spirit with ears that hear

Praise with a price is costly but it's ever so sweet
Leading to the place of honor, at our Master's feet

Trust

Life causes us to look for those that we can trust
But God alone has promised to walk with us

We search for answers as we travel life's road
Not convinced that Jesus alone will bear the load

As time passes by, our plans are often rearranged
Set aside, put on hold, and sometimes changed

We struggle to understand the challenges we face
Yet in our strength, we attempt to run the race

Still we must fix our eyes on the One who created it all
Fully submitting to His will and answering His call

The madness of the world must not be the norm
To its temporal pleasures, we must never conform

With an open ear, we will hear the Master's voice
And know that trusting Him is the wisest choice

When Jesus lives in us, we are never without help
But far from the cares of the world, we are kept

As we rest in Jesus, He causes every care to cease
With the promise of His unfailing love and His peace

In an uncertain world, God is faithful and just
Defending those who will give Him unwavering trust

The Call

God calls us to fix our eyes on things above
To fully rely on Him and receive His love

At the end of this life, our Savior we will meet
As prostrate we fall and worship at His feet

Then we will truly say that it has been worth it all
Rejoicing in the day that we answered His call

The last will be first and the first will be last
And shame from all sin will be in the past

Rejoicing will be heard on the streets of glory
As Jesus calls us home and completes the story

Keep oil in your lamps and watch for that day
For the coming of our Lord is not far away

The curtains of heaven will be opened wide
For the saints of God who've come to abide

As the day approaches, for Him our hearts burn
Desiring to meet Jesus, longing for His return

Share the message of hope, plead with the lost
For those who reject Jesus will pay a heavy cost

Lift up your eyes; see the Word of God unfold
As the splendors of heaven continue to be told

Many will not hear, but the trumpet will sound
Yet hidden in God, believers will be found

The table has been prepared for every invited guest
And the banquet before us is indeed heaven's best

Prepare for tomorrow, for all of eternity awaits
Forever with Jesus is just beyond heaven's gates

Choose Him now, for He has already chosen you
Let old things pass away and in Him be made new

May your name be sealed in the Lamb's Book of Life
For the Bridegroom awaits, and He longs for His wife

In the blink of an eye, we will be snatched away
To the presence of Jesus, for that's where we'll stay

So fix your eyes on Jesus, the One who matters most
As you prepare your heart to meet the heavenly host

God readies His watchmen; He sets them on the wall
Pleading for others to draw near and answer the call

Hidden Treasures

A message in the night caused me to wonder
Filling my mind, leaving much to ponder

Questioning this dream, daring to believe
That this much happiness I would receive

Looking to God and trusting His voice
Acknowledging Him, accepting His choice

My eyes are opened, and I discover God's plan
As wisdom is gained, I now understand

That which seemed certain is often changed
As wills are surrendered, plans are rearranged

Each moment holds a treasure, often tucked away
In glimpses from heaven, throughout each day

A pearl of great price many times is unseen
Its unspoiled beauty, we often fail to glean

Yet as we yield to God, He will gladly speak
Revealing hidden treasures, which we did not seek

The Presence of His Spirit

It's been a while, but few seem to notice that He's gone
Not welcomed, God left His church to function on its own

Saying the right words but missing the essence of Him
The brightness of His presence has now become dim

While many slept, God continued to plead His case
Longing for His children to come and seek His face

Where is the brokenness that once caused us to wail?
As we cried out for the lost and on our faces fell

A gathering without God's Spirit is no gathering at all
It's only man's traditions, if on God we do not call

Sadly, many do not miss the sweetness of God's presence
Not realizing that in all we do, He is the very essence

Prayer apart from God does not get beyond the ceiling
For it lacks God's power, and is only based on feeling

But as we are led by God and empowered from on high
The Holy Spirit will dwell, He will always be nearby

Break us Lord that we may be filled with You
Shake off complacency, give us a wider view

Fill us with Your Spirit, fill us with Your power
Help us to always walk humbly in this final hour

We are powerless, we are helpless apart from You
So come Holy Spirit, refresh us and fill us anew

About the Author

Janet Hanna started writing poetry from early childhood. As she spent time walking through the woods in Thomson, Georgia, she enjoyed God's creation. God began to reveal Himself through nature. Every tree that sprang up to the sky and every flower that bloomed showed evidence that God was real. Through people, places, and events, God began to reveal that He truly was the Maker of all things. And as time would progress, Janet would one day find out that all of God's creation had a story to tell.

Janet's life led her down several roads, as she ran from the call of God on her life. Still, all the while, there was a longing in her soul that nothing or no one could fill. However, on April 6, 1996, Janet came face-to-face with the unconditional love of God, through His Son Jesus Christ. Janet repented of her sins and accepted Jesus Christ as her Lord and Savior. Jesus Christ filled the void in her soul and continues to make Himself known to her. Janet was gloriously filled with the Spirit of God, and God's purpose for her life began and continues to unfold.

Janet holds an associate of arts degree in general studies from Brevard Community College. She also holds a bachelor's, master's, and doctorate of religious education from Evangelical Bible Seminary. She currently lives in Cocoa, Florida, with her son Jonathan.

Janet is very excited about her walk with God and looks forward to all that He has in store for the future. She prays that God's Spirit will lead all who are empty to be filled in the presence of Jesus Christ. To Him be all of the glory!